THE EUGÉNIE ROCHEROLLE SERIES

Intermediate Piano Solo

On the Jazzy Side

6 Original Solos by Eugénie Rocherolle

T0080121

ISBN 978-1-4234-7641-2

HAL•LEONARD®
CORPORATION

7777 W. BLUEMOUND RD. P.O. BOX 13819 MILWAUKEE, WI 53213

In Australia Contact:
Hal Leonard Australia Pty. Ltd.
4 Lentara Court
Cheltenham, Victoria, 3192 Australia
Email: ausadmin@halleonard.com.au

Visit Hal Leonard Online at
www.halleonard.com

HIGH FIVE!

By EUGÉNIE ROCHEROLLE

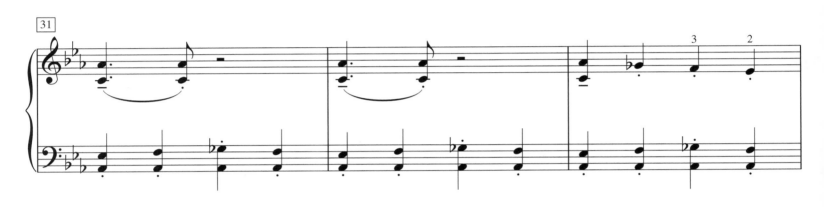

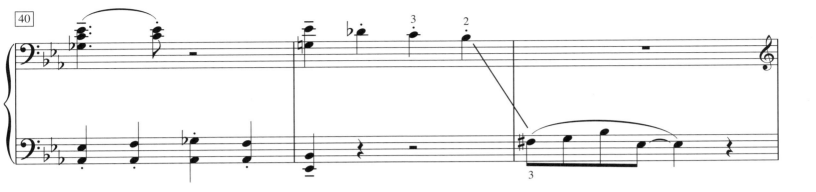

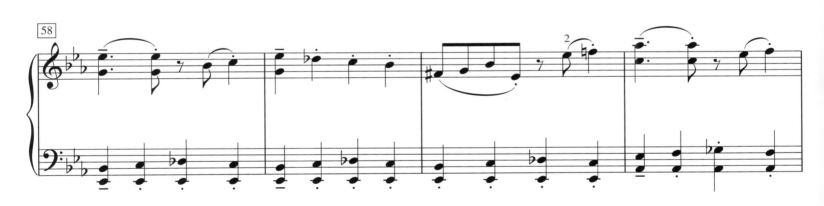

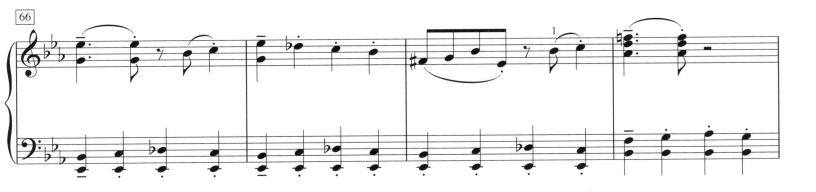

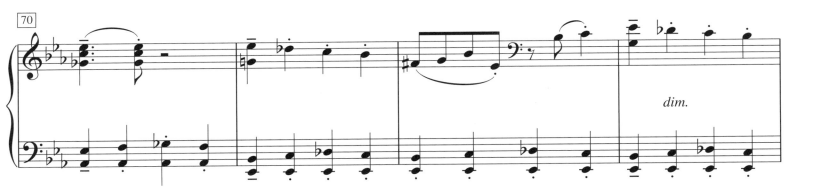

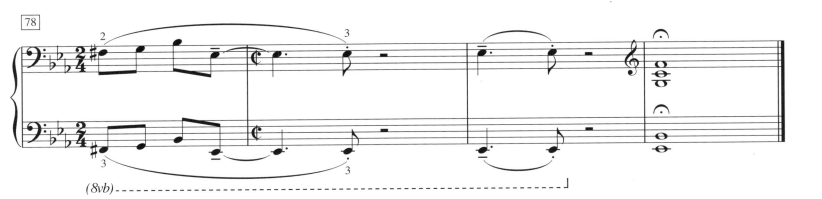

JUBILATION!

By EUGÉNIE ROCHEROLLE

Slower (♩ = 104)

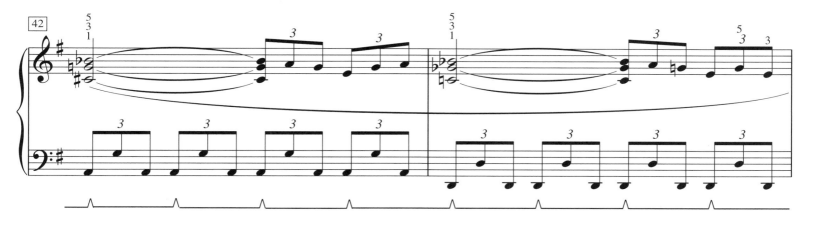

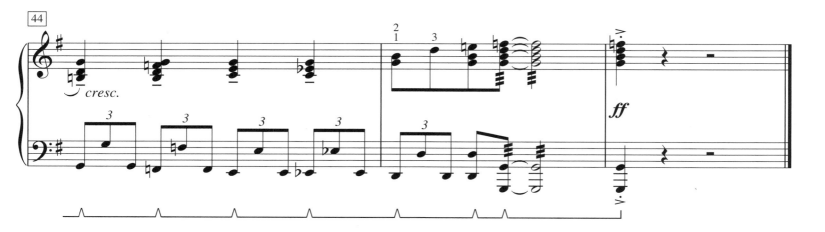

PRIME TIME

By EUGÉNIE ROCHEROLLE

Perky (♩ = 80)

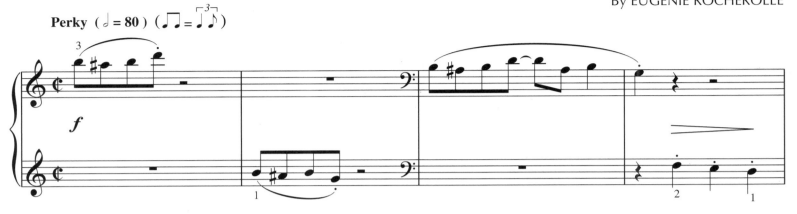

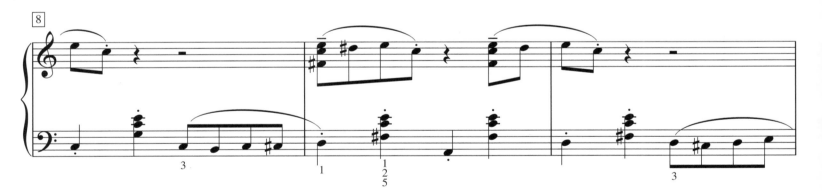

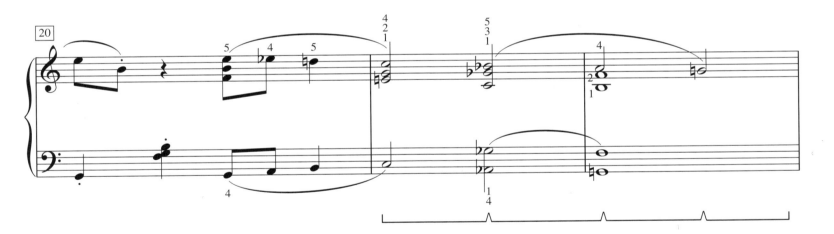

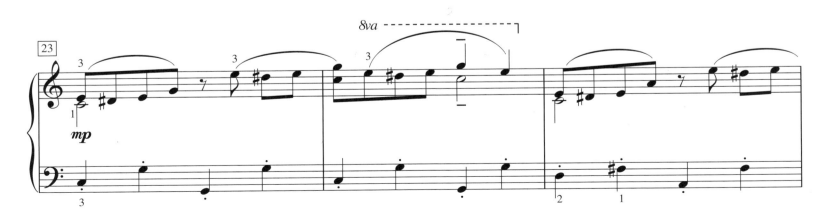

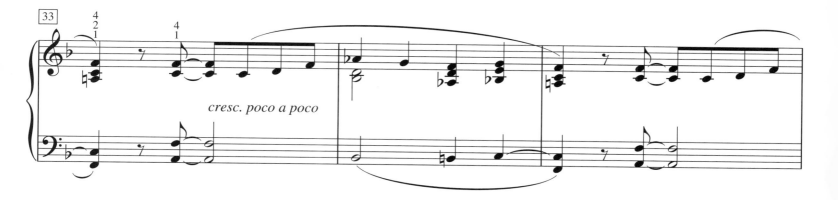

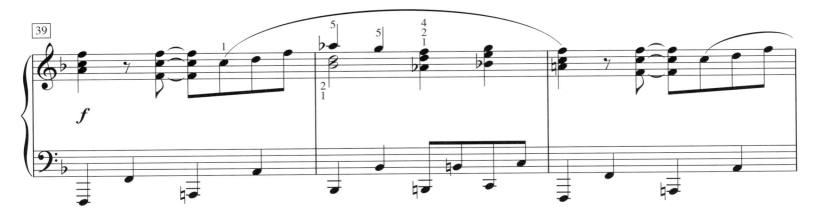

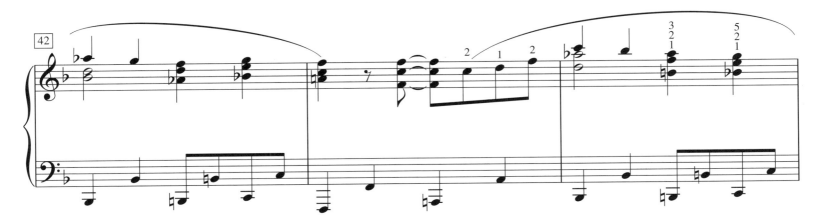

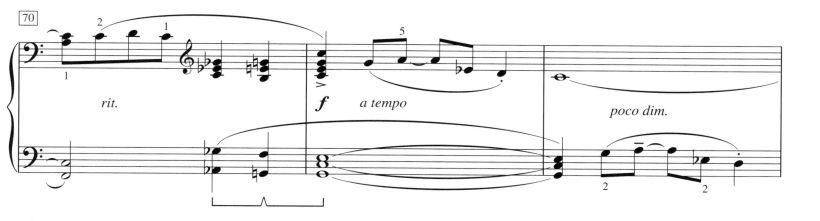

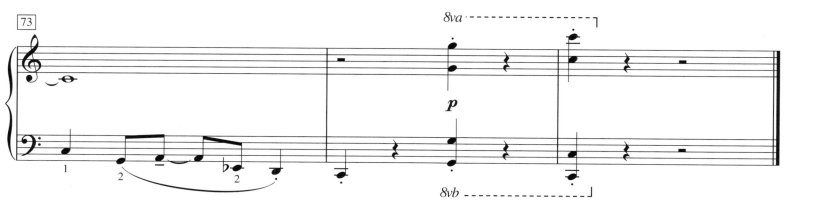

SMALL TOWN BLUES

By EUGÉNIE ROCHEROLLE

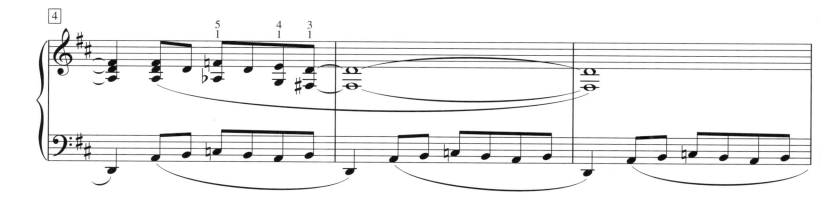

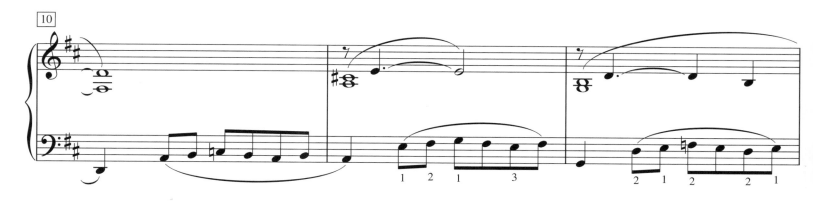

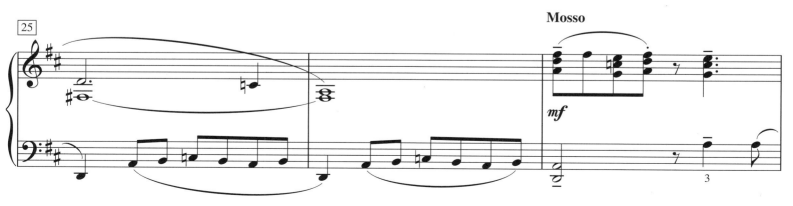

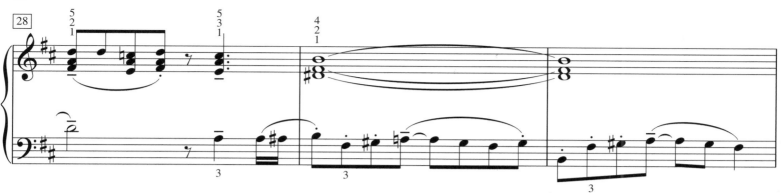

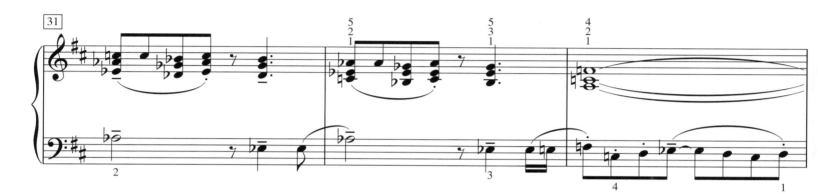

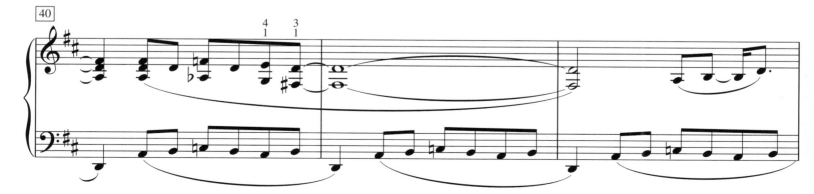

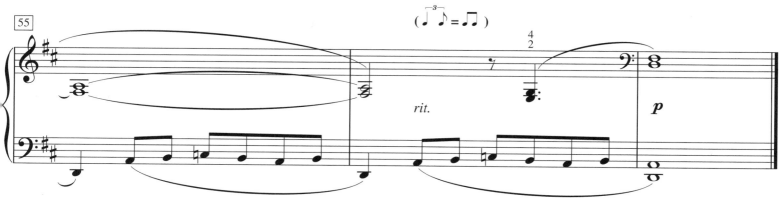

TRAVELIN' LIGHT

By EUGÉNIE ROCHEROLLE

With an easy swing ($\quad$ = 132)

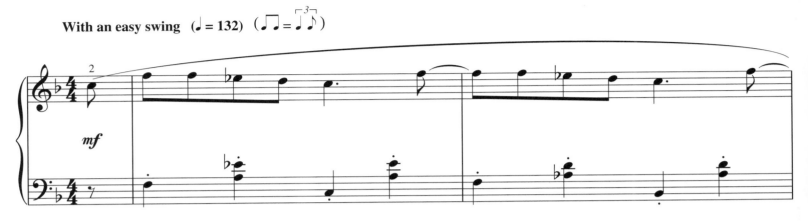

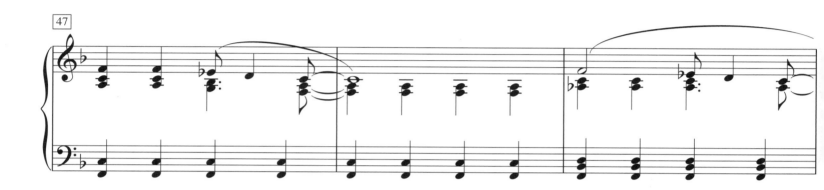

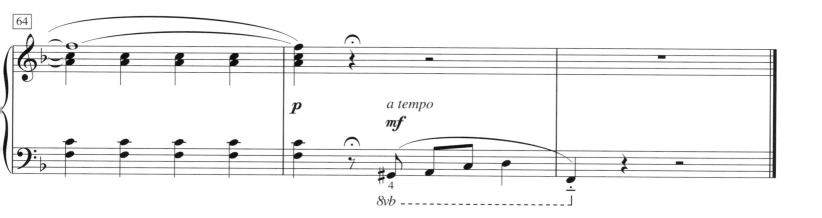

SMALL TALK

By EUGÉNIE ROCHEROLLE

Playfully (♩ = 92)

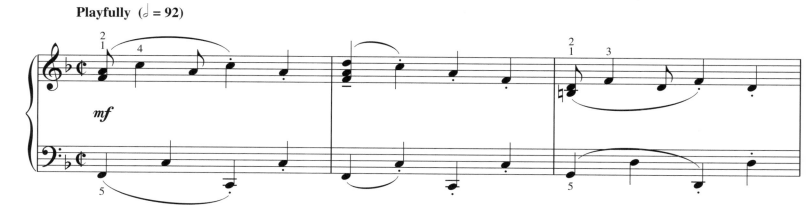

mf

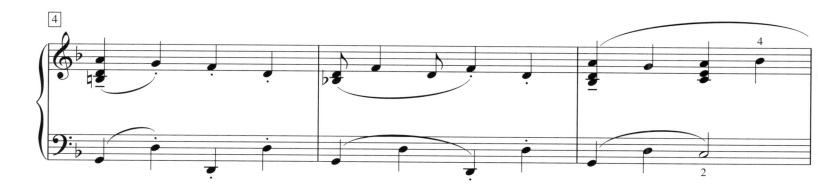

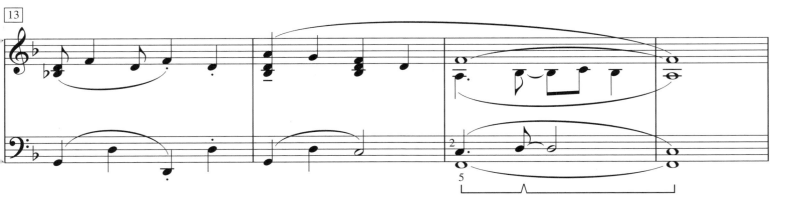

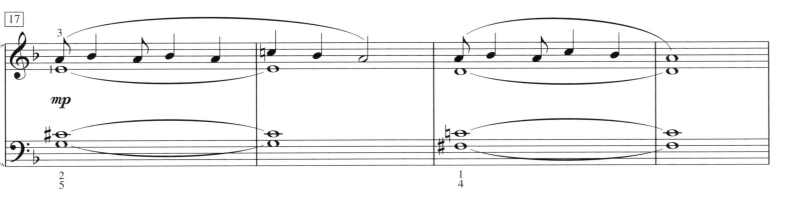

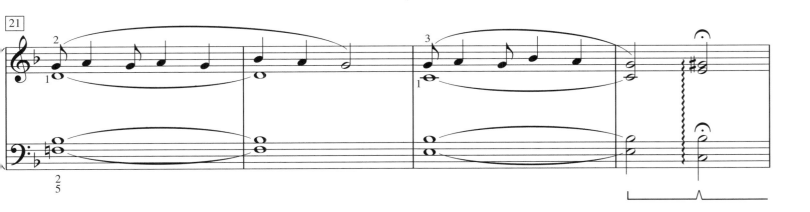

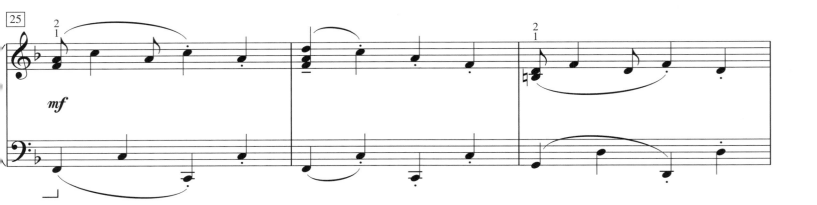

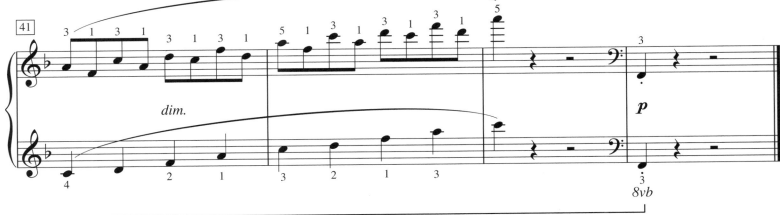

THE EUGÉNIE ROCHEROLLE SERIES

Offering both original compositions and popular arrangements, these stunning collections are ideal for intermediate-level pianists! Each book includes a companion CD with recordings performed by Ms. Rocherolle.

Candlelight Christmas
Eight traditional carols: Away in a Manger • Coventry Carol • Joseph Dearest, Joseph Mine • O Holy Night (duet) • O Little Town of Bethlehem • Silent Night • The Sleep of the Infant Jesus • What Child Is This?
00311808................$12.95

Recuerdos Hispanicos
Seven original solos: Brisas Isleñas (Island Breezes) • Dia de Fiesta (Holiday) • Un Amor Quebrado (A Lost Love) • Resonancias de España (Echoes of Spain) • Niña Bonita (Pretty Girl) • Fantasia del Mambo (Mambo Fantasy) • Cuentos del Matador (Tales of the Matador).
00311369................$12.95

Valses Sentimentales
Seven original solos: Bal Masque (Masked Ball) • Jardin de Thé (Tea Garden) • Le Long du Boulevard (Along the Boulevard) • Marché aux Fleurs (Flower Market) • Nuit sans Etoiles (Night Without Stars) • Palais Royale (Royal Palace) • Promenade á Deux (Strolling Together).
00311497................$12.95

Swingin' the Blues
Six blues originals: Back Street Blues • Big Shot Blues • Easy Walkin' Blues • Hometown Blues • Late Night Blues • Two-Way Blues.
00311445................$12.95

It's Me, O Lord
Nine traditional spirituals: Deep River • It's Me, O Lord • Nobody Knows De Trouble I See • Swing Low, Sweet Chariot • and more.
00311368................$12.95

Classic Jazz Standards
Ten beloved tunes: Blue Skies • Georgia on My Mind • Isn't It Romantic? • Lazy River • The Nearness of You • On the Sunny Side of the Street • Stardust • Stormy Weather • and more.
00311424................$12.95

ALSO BY EUGÉNIE ROCHEROLLE

The Beatles
Popular Songs Series
The top hits of the Beatles featured in this collection display a wide range of styles: stunning, lyrical arrangements, such as "Michelle," as well as incisively hip renditions of several of the Beatles' edgier tunes, as in "Revolution."
Intermediate Level
00296649 ....$9.95

Christmas Time Is Here
Duet for One Piano, Four Hands
Popular Songs Series
Six favorites: Christmas Time Is Here • Feliz Navidad • Here Comes Santa Claus (Right down Santa Claus Lane) • I'll Be Home for Christmas • Little Saint Nick • White Christmas.
Intermediate Level
00296614 ....$6.95

Jerome Kern Classics
Popular Songs Series
Students young and old will relish these sensitve stylings of enduring classics. Includes: All the Things You Are • Make Believe • Who? • and seven more.
Intermediate Level
00296577 ....$12.95

Melody Times Two
Classic Counter-Melodies for Two Pianos, Four Hands
Popular Songs Series
Includes two complete scores for performance. Songs: Baby, It's Cold Outside • Play a Simple Melody • Sam's Song • You're Just in Love.
Intermediate Level
00296360 ....$12.95

Jambalaya
A Portrait of Old New Orleans
Composer Showcase Series
This portrait of old New Orleans captures the lively and beautiful moods of this great city in its most elegant light. Eugénie's touching tribute to the city of her childhood is especially meaningful in the aftermath of hurricane Katrina. Alternating between a jazzy, upbeat style and lyrical warmth, the piece ends with a celebratory reference to "O When the Saints Go Marching In."

Piano Duo (2 Pianos, 4 Hands)
Includes two scores.
00296725 Intermediate Level $7.95

Piano Ensemble (2 Pianos, 8 Hands)
Score contains Piano I and Piano II duo parts. Two scores needed for rehearsal.
00296654 Intermediate Level $9.95

Piano Solo
00296712 Intermediate Level $4.95

Prime Time
Duet for One Piano, Four Hands
Showcase Solos Series
This striking 12-page duet was commissioned by the Music Educators of Greater Annapolis and debuted at their 2008 convention.
Intermediate Level
00296757 ....$3.95

HAL•LEONARD®

0409

COMPOSER SHOWCASE
HAL LEONARD STUDENT PIANO LIBRARY

This series showcases the varied talents of our **Hal Leonard Student Piano Library** family of composers.

Here is where you will find great original piano music by your favorite composers, including Phillip Keveren, Carol Klose, Jennifer Linn, Bill Boyd, and many others. Carefully graded for easy selection, each book contains gems that are certain to become tomorrow's classics!

EARLY ELEMENTARY

JAZZ PRELIMS
by Bill Boyd
HL00290032   12 Solos.......................$5.95

ELEMENTARY

JAZZ STARTERS I
by Bill Boyd
HL00290425   10 Solos.......................$6.95

JUST PINK
by Jennifer Linn
HL00296722   9 Solos.........................$5.95

MUSICAL MOODS
by Phillip Keveren
HL00296714   7 Solos.........................$5.95

PUPPY DOG TALES
by Deborah Brady
HL00296718   5 Solos.........................$6.95

LATE ELEMENTARY

CIRCUS SUITE
by Mona Rejino
HL00296665   5 Solos.........................$5.95

CORAL REEF SUITE
by Carol Klose
HL00296354   7 Solos.........................$5.95

IMAGINATIONS IN STYLE
by Bruce Berr
HL00290359   7 Solos.........................$5.95

JAZZ STARTERS II
by Bill Boyd
HL00290434   11 Solos.......................$6.95

JAZZ STARTERS III
by Bill Boyd
HL00290465   12 Solos.......................$6.95

LES PETITES IMAGES
by Jennifer Linn
HL00296664   7 Solos.........................$6.95

MOUSE ON A MIRROR
by Phillip Keveren
HL00296361   5 Solos.........................$6.95

PLAY THE BLUES!
by Luann Carman (Method Book)
HL00296357   10 Solos.......................$8.99

SHIFTY-EYED BLUES
by Phillip Keveren
HL00296374   5 Solos.........................$6.95

TEX-MEX REX
by Phillip Keveren
HL00296353   6 Solos.........................$5.95

THROUGHOUT THE YEAR
by Christos Tsitsaros
HL00296723   12 Duets.....................$6.95

THE TOYMAKER'S WORKSHOP
by Deborah Brady
HL00296513   5 Duets........................$5.95

TRADITIONAL CAROLS FOR TWO
arr. by Carol Klose
HL00296557   5 Duets........................$7.99

EARLY INTERMEDIATE

DANCES FROM AROUND THE WORLD
by Christos Tsitsaros
HL00296688   7 Solos.........................$6.95

FANCIFUL WALTZES
by Carol Klose
HL00296473   5 Solos.........................$7.95

JAZZ BITS AND PIECES
by Bill Boyd
HL00290312   11 Solos.......................$6.95

MONDAY'S CHILD
by Deborah Brady
HL00296373   7 Solos.........................$6.95

PORTRAITS IN STYLE
by Mona Rejino
HL00296507   6 Solos.........................$6.95

THINK JAZZ!
by Bill Boyd (Method Book)
HL00290417.......................................$9.95

THE TWELVE DAYS OF CHRISTMAS
arr. Deborah Brady
HL00296531   13 Solos.......................$6.95

WORLD GEMS
arr. Amy O'Grady (Piano Ens./2 Pianos, 8 Hands)
HL00296505   6 Folk Songs $6.95

INTERMEDIATE

AMERICAN IMPRESSIONS
by Jennifer Linn
HL00296471   6 Solos $7.95

ANIMAL TONE POEMS
by Michele Evans
HL00296439   10 Solos.......................$6.95

CHRISTMAS IMPRESSIONS
by Jennifer Linn
HL00296706   8 Solos.........................$6.95

CONCERTO FOR YOUNG PIANISTS
by Matthew Edwards (2 Pianos, 4 Hands)
HL00296356   Book/CD....................$16.95

CONCERTO NO. 2 IN G MAJOR
by Matthew Edwards (2 Pianos, 4 Hands)
HL00296670   3 Movements.............$16.95

DAKOTA DAYS
by Sondra Clark
HL00296521   5 Solos.........................$6.95

DESERT SUITE
by Carol Klose
HL00296667   6 Solos.........................$6.95

For full descriptions and song lists for the books listed here, and to view a complete list of titles in this series, please visit our website at **www.halleonard.com**

Prices, contents, & availability subject to change without notice.

FOR MORE INFORMATION, SEE YOUR LOCAL MUSIC DEALER,
OR WRITE TO:

FAVORITE CAROLS FOR TWO
arr. Sondra Clark
HL00296530   5 Duets........................$6.95

FLORIDA FANTASY SUITE
by Sondra Clark
HL00296766   3 Duets........................$7.95

ISLAND DELIGHTS
by Sondra Clark
HL00296666   4 Solos.........................$6.95

JAMBALAYA
by Eugénie Rocherolle (2 Pianos, 8 Hands)
HL00296654   Piano Ensemble............$9.95

JAZZ DELIGHTS
by Bill Boyd
HL00240435   11 Solos.......................$6.95

JAZZ FEST
by Bill Boyd
HL00240436   10 Solos.......................$6.95

JAZZ MOODS
by Tony Caramia
HL00296728   8 Solos.........................$6.95

JAZZ SKETCHES
by Bill Boyd
HL00220001   8 Solos.........................$6.95

LES PETITES IMPRESSIONS
by Jennifer Linn
HL00296355   6 Solos.........................$6.95

MELODY TIMES TWO
arr. by Eugénie Rocherolle
HL00296360   4 Duets.....................$12.95

MONDAY'S CHILD
(A CHILD'S BLESSINGS)
by Deborah Brady
HL00296373   7 Solos.........................$6.95

POETIC MOMENTS
by Christos Tsitsaros
HL00296403   8 Solos.........................$7.95

ROMP!
by Phillip Keveren
(Digital Ensemble/6 Keyboards, 6 Players)
HL00296549   Book/CD....................$9.95
HL00296548   Book/GM Disk $9.95

SONATINA HUMORESQUE
by Christos Tsitsaros
HL00296772   3 Movements...............$6.99

SONGS WITHOUT WORDS
by Christos Tsitsaros
HL00296506   9 Solos.........................$7.95

SUITE DREAMS
by Tony Caramia
HL00296775   4 Solos.........................$6.99

TALES OF MYSTERY
by Jennifer Linn
HL00296769   6 Solos.........................$7.99

THREE ODD METERS
by Sondra Clark (1 Piano, 4 Hands)
HL00296472   3 Duets $6.95

HAL•LEONARD®
CORPORATION
7777 W. BLUEMOUND RD. P.O. BOX 13819 MILWAUKEE, WI 53213

0109